1. MECOPP (Minority Ethnic Carers of People Project) was established in 2000 and provides a range of services to minority ethnic carers and those in receipt of informal care. The Gypsy/Traveller Carers' Project currently works in Edinburgh and the Lothians, Perth and Kinross and Mid and North Argyll. We work with Gypsy/Traveller carers of any age who live on sites, roadside camps and in housing.

Acknowledgements

Moving Minds was originally created as an exhibition for display during the Scottish Mental Health Arts and Film Festival, a Scotland-wide festival which uses the arts to challenge perceptions about mental health and promote wellbeing. For many contributors, participation in this creative process has already had a positive impact on wellbeing.

This book contains detailed narratives from individual Gypsy/Travellers and photographs from Chattery (*Our Lives in Bits and Bobs*), both parts of the *Moving Minds* exhibition. For Chattery each contributor was asked to choose a special object that could be held in the hand. Chattery is a Cant word for 'bits and bobs' and Cant is a traditional language still used by many Gypsy/Travellers in Scotland today.

The editors would like to thank all contributors and their families for their generosity of time and spirit without which neither the exhibition nor this book would have been possible. Thanks to the four Ls (Louise Macaulay, Linzi Ferguson, Lizzie Sosenko and Lucy Arnot), Kevin McKay, Emma-Jane Harrington and Suzanne Munday at MECOPP. We gratefully acknowledge the funders of the MECOPP Gypsy/Traveller Carers' Project – Scottish Government, Perth and Kinross council and NHS Lothian.

We are also grateful to Mary MacDonald for her meticulous editing and to Mary Fee, Colin Clark and Lesley Riddoch for their contributions and feedback. Thanks are also due to Linda Irvine, Dimitri Tsintjilonis, Jeanne Cannizzo, Edward Ross, Jo McFarlane and the late Richard Morran for their encouragement, support and helpful suggestions.

Lastly, but most importantly, we are indebted to all the Gypsy/Travellers who so candidly, and at times courageously, shared their memories, stories and mementos, not to mention their warmth and humour. Without them there would be no book.

Introduction

How do you think about your past, present and future? About your family, your friends and those close to you? About those people that you love and the people you have lost? How do you express yourself in times of frustration or times of happiness? What wee trinkets could you never imagine throwing out in a 'spring-clean' or even just misplacing for a few stolen hours?

This wonderful new book tells many such diverse stories from Scotland's Gypsy and Traveller population and captures particular moments in time that clearly matter. Important objects and mementos – the 'bits and bobs' of life – lead you into familiar worlds: art, poetry, anecdotes – and fine china – that will not fail to give you pause for reflection about the lives you are witnessing, the many faces which are looking out at you from the pages that you turn.

And it really is a 'page-turner' – for it is the struggle for humanity and dignity that won't fail to move you and touch your sense of justice and heartache. There is a deep pride and demand for respect that runs through this collection. To be sure, there is hurt and damage here as well – and the stories of recovery, redemption and faith will surely lift your spirits. You will also encounter many individual and unique lives on these roads, stretched out in front and always leading you home – a home, whether on wheels or not – that will always mark you as 'you'. For indeed, who are you one of? What will connect you to these encounters?

This is not just social history: the moments and memories, the hopes and fears, that are gathered here, tell us all something about ourselves and those around us. It is this individual and collective human need to connect with our past, present and future that helps us to make sense of who we really are.

Professor Colin Clark
University of the West of Scotland

Foreword

I was delighted to be asked to write this short foreword to the *Moving Minds* book.

My involvement with the Gypsy/Traveller community began when, as Convener of the Equal Opportunities Committee in the Scottish Parliament, we began inquiries into Gypsy/Travellers and care and Gypsy/Travellers and accommodation.

I consider myself hugely privileged to have been given the opportunity to meet Gypsy/Travellers from across Scotland, be welcomed into their homes, learn about their culture and be considered a friend.

Many myths and misconceptions exist about the Gypsy/Traveller community, all of them false and deeply offensive.

I was given the opportunity to learn about the traditional culture, language and craft of this warm and welcoming community.

The *Moving Minds* book wonderfully demonstrates their rich culture and heritage, and more importantly, the pride they have in their lifestyle and their determination to keep it alive.

The book will help dispel the myths and lack of understanding of this community and give the reader a vibrant insight into their lives.

I wish everyone involved every success and would like to put on record my gratitude to the Gypsy/Traveller community for sharing their lives with me.

Mary Fee MSP

Contents

'it's a GOOD life but a HARD life'

traditions

myths

p
r
o
p   u
o   **PROUD**
o
u   pride
d

proud

H
E   **DIFFICULT**
R
I   f r e e d o m
T
A   *BLESSED*
G   'a lot'
E   CONTENTMENT

F
R   frightened   c
E   *discrimination*   l
E   o
D   S   s   memories   marvellous   suffering
O   T   e   **family**
M   R   isolated   n
         E   e
         S   s   excellent   culture
         S   s
         F   camouflage   FREE
         U   happiness   difficult   HARD   outside
         L   *shifting*
                                                   pride, prejudice and respect

DOOM
PUBLIC HYSTERIA   air   e x c e l l e n t   *difficult*
                                                  story**TELLING**

'it's a great life when you are allowed'

Moving Minds

Gypsy/Travellers in Scotland

He Was Some Boy

I'm Patsy Stewart Hilton, a Scottish Traveller. I was a carer for my brother for nineteen years but I don't like to say carer, I was just Benny's sister, that's how it is with family. Aye, I was his sister, you could say he cared for me.

When we were wee, kids like, he was into this and that and me, being the oldest lassie, I kinda had to keep an eye on him. Benny was brought up to know he wisnae any different, there were eight of us and if Benny had done wrong, he got a skelp as well.

My father and mother wouldn't let him out of their sight: no school for him. When we were younger we'd pull in, pitch the tent up and one would go to the farm for straw, one for water, get things organised like gas bottles and a cuppa tea. So Benny would come with us to get firewood, we'd all get a bundle of sticks but he would lift a twig, that was Benny's sticks – one twig! He was some boy.

When everybody was travelling aboot, somebody said, "Have any of you seen John?"

And they'd say, "John? John who?"

"You ken Maggie and John with Benny."

Aye, it was Benny they knew you by.

In those days it was gate tents, the square ones. We lay on a straw bed. So we put straw in the back and the boys lay on the back bed, in the middle the lassies and then your mum and da lay in the front bed. Then there was a barricade at the front with the fire and the kettle. When you went to bed at night our father just lay and told you stories. Ah it was great, we just lay in bed listening to his stories. If a daddy-long-legs came in, it would be bouncing up and down on the canvas. My father used to lie whistling a pipe tune and it would be keeping time to the tune! That's the truth! My father used to just lie and say, "Look weans, watch, watch."

If I woke up during the night and I was thirsty I'd say, "Mum, mum. I'm thirsty."

"Well go out for the can."

Well, I'd climb over the top of them to get out, get past them, get the can and I'd go, "Ah there's nae water." But I couldn't go out in the blind dark looking for water, so I'd put the can doon and she'd say, "The kettle's there." Well years ago it was the big kettle; you'd put the tea in the kettle and you put the milk and sugar in and just stir it and pour it out.

She'd say, "Well the kettle's there, see if there is any tea left." So I'd lift the big kettle.

"Oh there's tea there." But when I put the spout to my mooth I'd keep my teeth closed 'cause I'd be getting tea leaves! Then I'd be satisfied and back to bed. And you'd be picking tea leaves off your teeth but you werenae caring 'cause you got a drink. Aye those were the days.

We were down in England, worked for the District Council for about nine years running sites. Dad took no well so we got time off our work to come up – he really wisnae well, and mum was a semi-invalid herself and it was hard for her coping with Benny even when dad was there. After we went back down Matt, my man, and I kept thinking about mum trying to cope and then we got word she wisnae well – so Matt says, "Ah come on Patsy we'll just go back up home." We rented a house and I came in the morning and Matt did his own thing away hawking and that. But mum got a lot worse, my sister took her to England and she died there but she always said, "If anything ever happens to me don't let my boy go over the border."

So we just stayed on in mum's house because I didn't want to upset Benny too much ye know: losing his mum and his dad. I'll no tell a lie 'cause I was finding it hard at first to cope with Benny 'cause nobody would come. You couldn't get anybody up to talk to, to say look he's this, he's that, is there anything I can get to help with him? They kept saying no.

A few years on when he was starting to get a bit uneasy on his feet, I would walk a wee bit with him then he'd say, "No, Patsy, no Patsy," and I'd have to take him back to the car. I got an NHS wheelchair for him but

Dad, Benny and Mum

I couldnae lift it. Everytime I went out if I seen a bloke passing I would say, "Excuse me could you give me a wee bit of help."

I got a catalogue one day through the door: was looking through it and thought, oh there's wheelchairs that look light. I thought, wait a minute I am going to phone social services to see if they could give me a wee help: since I was on my own by then.

They told me a gentleman had died and left some money to be used for people like Benny. A wee while later she phoned me back and said, "Mrs Hilton, good news, I've received the cheque for the wheelchair. That's good news, isn't it?" But she said she had bad news as well, "I've to oversee the spending of the money."

She made me feel as if I was a con woman, just the lowest of the low. She knew I was upset and I just said, "Best thing to do is you just keep the cheque, I don't want it," and I put the phone down.

About five minutes later she phoned back and says, "Look I'm awfully sorry about that, I'll send you the cheque out."

I sent away for the wheelchair and light as a feather it was: he loved it. I think that's about the dearest thing he ever got off social services.

Asking for help for me, maybe for all

Travellers, it's hard to say I cannae manage. I was scared to say too much because you're on a thin line. What I mean is if I ask for too much they'll say I'm not able to cope, "We'll have to put him in a care home."

And the thing my mother always said was, "If anything ever happens to me, dinnae put my laddie in a home." She always said that. Benny was her second oldest and born the way he was, we thought with weans like that, they need to be in among their own family.

In the end he was getting his days and nights mixed up and I had to apply for somebody to come in and give me a wee help 'cause it was getting to the stage where it was hard to get him lifted; to go to the toilet; to put him back into the bed; to get him washed in the morning. He wouldn't go in the shower, he was panicky with water, he would just scream the place down. So I thought I'm not going to put him through that torture, I'll just take a basin into the room and wash his body that way.

I got a social worker up here and she said,

"Mrs Hilton, we've had a meeting about Benny. We're going to send you out a carer."

I said, "I don't think one carer will be enough. I know him, I can kind of cope with it on my own but you'd need two carers to come out." But she knew best.

So they sent one and she went into the room and quickly says, "Mrs Hilton could you come out and give me a wee help?" So anyway they finally gave me two carers for him.

But one day, I was in here and they got him up, took him into the loo and I thought, they're taking an awfully long time. So I got up and went in and this is the truth, they had Benny stripped naked. Now there was nae heating on in the toilet and they had Benny in there, stripped naked sitting on the toilet and the man standing yabbing away to the other one. I looked in and I lost it, I may as well tell you, I said, "Excuse me, what are you doing?"

"Eh, I'm washing him," he said.

I said, "No you are not, you're not washing

my brother in here sitting on a toilet. He's a human being, he's not an animal."

Thankfully, that was the only time, usually the lassies that used to come were awfy, awfy good with him. Five days a week they came but no at the weekend 'cause of cutbacks. I cannae remember how it came about but a couple over the road from Romania, she came to the door one day. I gave her a cuppa and we were sitting talking away and it all came oot about the carers only coming five days a week. She says, "I will come and help you," but I said it disnae matter. You know I offered that woman payment but she wouldn't take it. I stuck it in her pocket, she took it back out and stuck it on the mantelpiece.

Benny loved Santa, he truly believed in Santa. He even brought Asda to a standstill – we were in to do a bit of shopping, I saw they had a Santa and thought, oh we're going to have fun! By then his eyesight was pretty bad but he got his eye on this red thing coming down the aisle and shouts, "Santa, oh Santa." Santa just looked at him and must have thought, oh God, is he alright?

When he did pass away it was bad, it was snowing, I knew he wisnae well, he just lay on the bed and I would go into him and say, "Oh look it's snowing, it won't be long now for Santa." The doctor said he'd taken pneumonia. I says, "What can I dae for him? I'm trying to do my best, what can I dae for him?"

He says, "Listen, there's no much you can do, you're doing all you can. He'll not know anything and just slip away."

It was ten o'clock at night, that was the time he passed away, phoned the doctor, he came, sounded him and said, "Yes he's gone." He was sitting talking to me and asking questions about whether I'd ever had help with him. Then he says, "You know Mrs. Hilton he's a really, really good age at seventy-four to have lived that long." You see Benny was only supposed to live till he was five.

Patsy Stewart Hilton

By Invitation Only.
Shamus McPhee
Watercolour 2003

My Secret

My secret
Staying in a house
has made things easier
for me and my family
hot and cold running water.
I feel I am dreaming
Knowing that I am being treated
like a normal person.
Kids going to school
Makes me feel great
Knowing they are learning
You never know what they may become
Doctors, nurses, vet, even a lawyer.
How great this would be
To my family and me.
For you see
I am keeping a secret
From the country people who surround me
I am from Travelling People.
No need to rock the boat
And go back to the old ways
Country people calling my children
dirty names, throwing stones
not getting allowed to use public buildings.

Worst of all,
Not getting taken on by a doctor
Specially when one has a child
Who needs around-the-clock treatment.
My secret
Staying in a house
Has given me the same equal rights as everyone else.
So I stick out my chin,
And smile and bear it,
Hiding away my real feelings.
Staying in a house
The downside is
Not showing my true feelings.
Not travelling the roads
With my friends and family
Or just staying outside
Below the stars at night.
It's a shame I need to lie
And cover up who I am
Just so I can get
A peaceful life, equal rights
Like the country people around me.

Lizzie Johnstone

Crown Derby Jug

When I was a child and visiting the Town Moor Fair in Newcastle, my mum bought a full set of Crown Derby and we were on our way home. My parents kept telling me to be quiet, "Shhh!!" The next thing the caravan overtook us, because it had jumped the ball, and flew into a ditch. This jug is the only thing that was left, the rest was sugar!

Christina

Gutted

I've been working since I was fifteen, I'm twenty-five now, in care homes, shops and restaurants. Most of the time people didn't know I was a Traveller and everything was fine. And when they found out that I was a Traveller I was either made redundant or they told me I wasn't needed any more.

For instance, there was one time I was working in a restaurant, and the manager who runs it, he stayed just up from the site where I live. One day his wife was on the bus and saw me get on at the bus-stop near the site and she was staring at me. And the next day, the supervisor came up to me and said, "We've got very few hours, we're going to have to let you go, that was your trial over." The trial only lasted a couple of days, she said that from the start, but I'd been working about three months by then.

I was just pure gutted, I felt like crying. I know for a fact that it was because the manager's wife had seen where I came from, it was the site. And recently I applied for a job with a carer organisation. I went for the interview before the application got sent in, it all went well and they basically asked me how many hours are you willing to do, are you willing to do this, and they wrote all these notes, shook my hand, and they said, "Get your details to us as soon as possible and we'll get back to you." She said it to me about three times, "Fill in the application form and send it off." They seemed really keen. They were even willing to give me a company car, 'cause I'd just turned twenty-five, and I was suitable for it because of the insurance. But after they got the application, I heard nothing, I'm sure it was when they seen the site address.

That's happened before when I've had to use another address just to get work, like I used Flat One and then the site address. That worked for a wee while, no problem, getting my pay slips and application forms; it was fine. Then that last application I put in, I used Pitch One and the site address and

that was when I never got the job. I mean it's meant to be equal opportunities. I just felt useless and really, really worthless, no good for nothing and just gutted.

I've got low self-esteem, and not got very much confidence as it is and that just knocked whatever confidence I did have. She didn't really give me a chance. If she had given me that one chance, I'd have proved I can work but it's like she just saw Traveller site and made up her mind.

I've got plenty of experience of caring, mainly 'cause I've got a disabled sister. She's twenty-one now and I've lived with her all my life. I do a lot of help at home, caring for her. Also I had a grandad, he was in a nursing home near where I live for eleven years, and he used to come to us a few times a week. He was in a wheelchair 'cause he'd had a stroke three times and was paralysed on one side. So I had a lot of experience with that kind of caring. I suppose I've got a lot of respect for older people, just want to make them happy,

Margaret and Fiona MacDonald

'cause they're so lonely.

I was a home carer with older people last year, but I had to leave that. I wasn't able to do that job after what happened. I was on a tea break one evening and I was walking along the street and I was approached by two girls and they attacked me for no reason, one of them stabbed me in the leg, they tried to get me in the neck. I was really, really shocked, the police couldn't get a word from me, I had to be taken to hospital for the night. They caught the girl as she was known to the police for carrying blades, and she'd been in jail before. When she got to court she got over a year 'cause there'd been other attacks. She's out just now, so I'm still kinda edgy, walking the streets, in case I bump into her, 'cause I have done twice and I just run. The way I feel, I can't describe it when I see her, I just run back to the car and lock myself in.

I don't think I've been the same person after that happened. I was really depressed and staying in all the time. I didn't want to go out at all, just sitting crying on my own. I got some help from Victim Support, and my GP, she was quite good as well. I'm starting to get back to my normal self a bit more now but I'm not as cheerful and happy as I used to be, 'cause I always thought this would never happen to me. And just like that, a flash, but in the long-term it has affected me big time.

I keep everything in. I've been diagnosed with anxiety, depression and low mood, and I've not been able to talk to anyone, not even my own family. My GP told me to start talking about it with Victim Support, but I just keep everything in. And I was having nightmares and waking up in cold sweats. But recently I've been starting to open up a wee bit, my sister's back home and that has helped a bit. That's the key, talking, opening up, but it isn't easy.

I don't really like to talk about these kinds of things, suppose I just keep it to myself, but that's no right 'cause then it gets worse, I know that myself: I've been in a bad way. It just totally knocked my confidence and I wasn't really that much confident anyway, I had a wee bit but that just knocked it completely. And then with the job stuff, that made it worse; they won't even give me a chance and that's not fair.

Fiona MacDonald

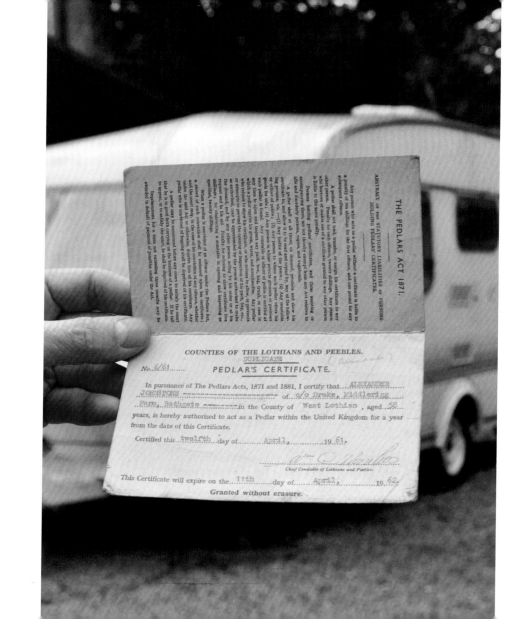

Pedlar's Certificate

The permit to me is important because it shows how certain groups are targeted for removal. You become a leper colony.

Shamus

Double Dykes Caravan Site, Perth

Where Did They Go?

There have been Travellers camping here in this area for over one hundred years. Camps for Travellers to stay on permanently in Perth have been looked at from the 1940s through to the 1970s.

In the 1980s there was a debate about where a site would be built. There were protests, news articles and objections against the site, saying:

"Is the local population going to be swamped by the tinker element?"

"Where are the children of these families to be educated. Not the village school I trust?"

"Villagers to fight travelling site plan."

"They behave as outlaws."

"Who will be prepared to live on the doorstep of this eyesore?"

"... there will be the usual filth, scrap metal and general rubbish ..."

"We are extremely concerned about the effect on our property in terms of theft, break-ins, etc. which will inevitably occur if these people are sited next to ..."

I read these words and it is strange to think they are talking about me and I was only nine-years-old.

Double Dykes finally opened in late 1982. It was built for one reason and that was to get the sixty families who were staying on 'the old road' off, so they could build the new Western bypass.

Newspapers at the time said there were a hundred families staying in the Perth area. Twenty pitches were provided at Double Dykes, the other families were made to move. Where did the rest of the Travellers go? Thirty years later there are still only twenty pitches, they didn't plan for growth in the Gypsy/Traveller community as they do for other communities. If there weren't enough pitches then, is it any wonder families have to 'double up' now? Double Dykes has been overcrowded since day one.

The fight to upgrade Double Dykes started about five years after it opened; due

"What is good about these two photos is that they show all the different types of accommodation used by Travellers in the 1960s – caravans, huts and bow camps."

to a lack of repairs the portacabins started to fall apart. Ever since it seems we've been fighting to get living conditions on the site improved. After many complaints and a long, long battle we finally got all the chalets on this site in 2008.

That's my message – the council can be good and helpful if they want but not if you are a Traveller living on a site. It took a lot of hard work, and funding from elsewhere, to get the improvements on Double Dykes. The rent here is over £100 a week, the highest in Scotland I think.

I am a full-time carer for my mother. I thought being a carer was about caring for someone, I didn't realise it was also about taking on the role of fighting the council. This long struggle has taken me away from being a carer, I have written hundreds of letters, been to councillors, the Citizens Advice Bureau, MSPs, because I don't give up. Everything I do, I've been advised to do and I follow this advice. This has seriously

Fiona Townsley with some of her correspondence and research papers

impacted on my ability to care for my parents.

It has affected my own health too, increasing the stress levels. I feel bullied and harassed by the council because I have challenged the way they view Travellers. It's now 2014, and we are still being treated like second-class citizens. Believe me at times I wish I could shut up but if we stop complaining nothing will change.

Fiona Townsley

Keep Very Quiet

WELL, the man has the position of the head of the family so that's where he has to be the strongest. Depression could crumble a man to his knees but it's not really heard of. It's real and it happens but it's not heard of, not exposed, nobody knows about it. It must be a thousand times harder on a man than a woman because there's so much responsibility on the man that he can't afford to crumble, he can't afford to have these illnesses but I know they do; it's just they are kept very quiet.

Georgia

Frying Pan

This is my mammy's frying pan, it's forty-two-years-old, forty-two years and frying the bacon still. The wean's daddy he engraved that dancing salmon on it with a darning needle that had been trimmed at the top. All the money in the lottery couldn't buy it.

Isa

Half A Trelaver

When I first went to the jail there was a wee bit of conflict about it. People didnae want to have anything to dae wi' you, things like that. Twenty I was when I first went. At Polmont the younger ones were just wee ringtails, but when I went to the bigger jail,

that was a different story. I thought, in a way it was like school, I'm in for it now. There's just going to be a heap of carry-on. They'll be going on at me 'Gypo' this and 'Gypo' that. The way I dealt with it was to come oot with it straight away. A lot of them know just by the way I talk, the way I act. I telt boys, "Aye look, I'm a Traveller and I hope yous havenae got a problem wi' it." The boys were alright about it.

See being a Traveller and being put to prison is, how can I put it, is just physical, mental torture. It's like being a lion: you get taken out of your domain and put in a cage. In a way this hoose is like a cage to me too. See looking at these four walls constantly, you've only got one windae. If I was in the trailer, the caravan as the boys from the hooses call it, I've got windaes all roond aboot me constantly and I can hook on whenever I want. I can come and go as I please, but see being in prison and being stuck into that routine, I've never been in a routine in my life but in the prison it's up in the morning, breakfast, after your breakfast, shower, after your shower, go to your work. See that routine way of going on, it's just a dark horrible feeling.

In fact I found in the prison the officers, the screws as we call them, they were more childish than the cons. Just petty wee things. I got put in solitary for what we call people in hooses, some of us Travellers call them scaldies. Well something happened with a family visit and they double-booked the visit but they gied me confirmation; you keep that slip so you've got a bit of proof. I went doon the next day and he says "Where are you going?"

I says, "You booked my visit." He point blank told me he didnae, even though I had my slip.

My granny is disabled and she's coming nearly two hundred mile with my mother, who was not too well, to bring my daughter to visit me out of the goodness of their hearts, and he's telling me I've no got a visit. I got a wee bit annoyed and so they got three or four of them aboot me and they locked me up. One of the officers – the boy was alright tae – he says, "Look Tom, John [the officer] will be back to see you in a minute."

I says, "Tell that scaldie no to come back near me." He went back and told him, "You better not go back near him because he's going to scald you."

When everyone else was oot I calmed doon, sat back and thought nothing aboot it. Next thing I heard was rumble, rumble, rumble. I thought something's going on here, so I got myself up against the wall. "Right come on then," he says and I said, "Four of yous? Yous are not taking me to the governor. Yous are taking me to the digger." The digger's solitary. So I'm sitting in the digger over the weekend and I'm thinking what's this aboot? So I went up in front of the governor, "You told an officer not to come back to you or you'd

scald him."

"No," I says, "I called him a scaldie. Tell that scaldie no to come near me." So I explained to him but he took it his officer's way. So just for calling somebody a scaldie I got put in the digger.

My wee girl she's fantastic. Going to prison was a big thing aboot her but now she's made me make a 'pinky promise'. She says, "You're not going to be a bad boy again are you dad?" So I've promised her, pinky promised in fact, that I'm not going to be a bad boy.

She's eight-year-old but she's got an eighteen-year-old heid on her, she has full-scale conversations with my gran. She's clued up that way. She's got me on the straight and narrow now but she muddles her words up sometimes. So the wean came up to me and said, "Mum said you're a Gypsy,"

I said, "I'm a Traveller,"

"You're a what?" So she sat and listened as I explained it to her and it was good for me to see the smile on her face because she was always hearing about what I was and that. After the conversation she was happy about it, so she went, "So what does that make me then? Am I like you or am I like my mammy?"

I says, "You've got the best of both worlds, baby girl, because you're half and half,"

"So I'm half a Trelaver,"

"No baby girl it's Traveller!" See when she seen me laughing she couldnae help herself but because it makes me laugh she comes oot with it all the time.

Her granny learns her all these Cant words 'barry', 'gadgie' and all this and it's brilliant. She'll go back hame and up the toon and she'll say, "Stall yer mangin mum," meaning, watch what you're saying mum, people's listening to you. Her mother will go, "What? What are you talking about?" Her mother's not got a clue. Oh she cracks me up, she's brilliant that way! She tells them all at school, "I'm a half a Trelaver." So she's happy with it all and takes it in her stride.

Tom 'Winky' Devers

Dead Man's Penny

It was important to my husband because it was his uncle's and then it was passed on to his dad and when his dad died, it was passed on to him and now I am going to probably pass it on to my daughter's wee one, called Jackie like him, and from there it will go on down the line. Now my father-in-law's uncle John was out in Italy. He was fighting. He was just going on eighteen when he was killed. Quite a lot of Gypsy/Travellers lost their lives quite young, going in the army quite young you know. Some of them fourteen, fifteen. My great-grandfather he was in the Boer War and his nephew was in with him. My great-grandfather came home but the nephew didn't. He was only fifteen-and-a-half.

Bella

Summer Travelling

Every chance I get I take photos. I have got hundreds, I mean hundreds of albums. Old ones and recent ones. Over your lifetime photos they're there, they tell you a story. You know you've always got that to look back on. You can always look back at photos and reminisce, the good times and bad times, you know.

This picture is of my twin daughters. That was the first time I ever got to hold them out of the incubators. It was very emotional, a very emotional day and the older one, Ashley, she was actually born with a tooth. And there was a wee Irish nurse who was in the hospital, she said it was very, very lucky. I've still got the tooth. They were four weeks in the incubator and seven weeks in total in the hospital. It was very hard, being able to see them but not being able to touch them, hold them you know. I just wanted to squeeze them and not give them back. They're now ten, and wild. Oh my goodness they keep you on

your feet. You'd have to be an athlete to keep up with Ashley and Shannon.

Unfortunately when they were three that's when we had to move out of the site into a house and they had just started nursery at Lochnell. It's mostly for Ashley and

Shannon's sake because with the house they've got the school with special needs. They need physio, speech therapy and occupational therapy.

Even though they were young they remember being uprooted, you know, from what they were used to and put into a house. You don't get so much communication when you live in a house. It's more isolated even though family visit and you go and visit them you still feel like you're in an alien environment – not what you're used to.

This photo is my son William, it was taken during the time that we were staying on Mull. We stayed there for three years and one of my husband's mates came up in the morning and asked if William would like to go and sit on the turtle. So it was about seven o'clock in the morning and we came down to the pier and he just sat on this ginormous turtle's back. It came in from a warmer climate and it got landed in the nets of a Mull fishing boat.

I never actually went to Mull till I started going with William but then we went back to Mull for a lot of years. Sometimes the people there could be a bit clannish, you know, and keep themselves to themselves. But there was a lot of nice people, it was the same as everywhere else, you get the good and the bad. Yeah it was good. His family travelled all the islands mostly Skye, Tiree, Uist, Stornoway, all the islands. Aye, I wasn't much of an islander until I met Willie.

For Ashley and Shannon I think it is

very important to get the chance to spend the summer travelling – they get to meet old friends and made some new friends this year, rather than being in the house. Just being on the campsite and meeting people you hadn't seen all year and knowing that you're not going to see them till next year.

It's not actually the way Travellers used to be, only that six weeks of the year. When we were younger you'd be travelling all year to different places and camps. I remember staying into Campbeltown and it was autumn time, and half the tent was collapsing wi' hazelnuts, because we were staying in a hazel wood. I don't know what the people on the bus used to think, seeing us kids walking out of the wood every morning to catch the bus to go to the high school. But one morning I went to the high school with a pair of tights full of hazelnuts and me and my sister sold them for pocket money during dinner times. We earned a few quid.

Betsy MacDonald

It's A Shame

The world is
a very big place
which holds so many
beautiful wonderful things.
It's a shame
people can't be the same
when they see
Travelling People.

Lizzie Johnstone

Ring

This ring is called a 'keeper' – a keeper for life. I got it as a sixteenth birthday present from my da. He's had seven boys and bought one for each of us when we turned sixteen.

Buller

A Godsend

I am Susan and I live on Double Dykes site in Perth. I had to start using a wheelchair about two-and-a-half years ago after I had to get a leg amputated. That was because of vascular problems – caused partly by myself neglecting my own health by being reluctant to ask for health advice. But when I did finally go to the doctor, maybe they kept me hanging on a long time too.

I was in hospital for four weeks, I got home and that's when my problems really started. I now had no independent access to my own chalet, and that's my home.

It took eleven months just to get the step outside changed; until then I had to be carried up and down the stairs by family members. At first I actually refused the new steps because I knew they weren't suitable. What I needed was a ramp. But I was told, "It is that or nothing."

I fell about six or seven times with those steps: it is awkward going down with a leg that doesn't bend at the knee. Once I even fell in front of the site warden and him and a workman had to lift me: it was so embarrassing, it really was.

One day my husband went out and accidentally left the toaster on, I was lying on the bed and the fire alarm went off. I realised I wasn't going to get out if there was a fire, I was trapped, and that night I was dreaming about it and took a panic attack which ended up in me being hospitalised. I actually think you have to experience something like that to realise how frightening it can be, knowing you wouldn't be able to get out.

After that I did think about a house as I thought that was my only option even after living on the site since 1984, but I really didn't want to move into a house.

For me the worst thing about getting anything from the disability people is the waiting, and usually no communication – even if they would just keep in touch or say they are working on it. It makes you feel like they've forgotten you. If you phone it's

Susan Townsley on the lift into her chalet

a machine and they don't return calls. But recently I have been speaking at the Scottish Parliament and now they seem to keep in touch. I hadn't seen the occupational therapist for over a year but now she's in contact regularly.

When they built sites for Travellers they didn't think about someone with a disability or an old person. My mother lived on the site for over fifteen years but had eventually to go into a house, at seventy-four, away from her family and community, even though that was the time she needed us most.

We do get treated differently: I think Travellers are made to feel grateful for what little we've got, even though half the time it is half a job. When we were asking for a ramp I was told, "Do you not think the council has spent enough on this site?" – I was made to feel it was my fault.

For me, that lift is a Godsend, after waiting near on two years. Ma man says he hardly sees me now, I'm always away somewhere.

Susan Townsley

A Thorn In The Side

I'm a Scottish Gypsy/Traveller, a native of Pitlochry brought up on this site. I'm also a teacher of Gaelic and English and to a lesser extent Media Studies. I've also done television training and I've studied Human Rights at Strasburg. None of which has been any good to me because the essential thing is I'm a Gypsy/Traveller and therefore it doesn't matter how many bits of paper you have.

At the moment I'm looking after an elder family member but we've always done that. When we were children growing up, we used to do errands for old people around the site, you'd maybe get a penny for a sweetie if you went and got the shopping or helped them with something they couldn't do. I think you are taught as you grow up in a Gypsy/Traveller family to look after each other and particularly the elderly. There's more respect for the elderly. I think that's something that's always been. It's just a skill you grow up with from a very early age. It's not something you have to learn, making it easier in one respect. What makes it more difficult is all the problems you encounter with bureaucrats, trying to access services, basic infrastructure, things that other people take for granted.

If the benefit office has stopped his benefit, or if my benefit is stopped for some reason, you can't get through on the mobile. You put £10 in and you're still on the answering machine. You can't afford to keep doing that and the longer you're on a phone and getting no answer, the more tense and irritated you become. I don't think that helps at all and it certainly hasn't helped me because I've had severe problems with oesophagitis and stomach acidity and that's been exacerbated since I became a carer. I think that's because you're getting tense a lot more without realising it. That's the sort of physical thing with it. Spiritually and mentally, you know, it's frustrating that I can't get out to do things that I'd like to do, like the campaigning stuff I've always done.

To counteract that, I use what spare time I can fit in, if he's resting, for my writing. I've been writing an autobiographical account of growing up, getting jobs as a teacher in areas where they didn't know I was a Traveller and what actually happened in one school when they found out. I was put in a boys' toilet that was disused, with no heating, to work in and then a cupboard with no light, to teach my higher class. It was totally humiliating for a teacher to be treated like that. My friend who has published tons of books is wanting me to go back and finish the *Tinker Teacher* one which is autobiographical but I prefer doing the thrillers because it's more of a flight of the imagination. As an English teacher I know that if you do it in a more entertaining way it's more likely to catch attention rather than simply laying the facts bare.

I still have my culture, they can't take that away from me. If you want to practise your language and practise your culture, you'll find a way to do it and they won't be able to stop you. I think that really is a thorn in the side of the authorities and probably why I've never had any work out of twenty-six applications in this area over twenty-two years because I've always identified with my culture. That's not something that's just going to be airbrushed from history if we keep it alive. To me that's positive.

Roseanna McPhee

Gold Earrings

My twin girls used to bite on these when they were teething, cut quite a few teeth on them they did. It was hard to get them off them. You can still see the teeth marks to this day.

Betsy

Libby's daughter, Mirren

It's Like *Groundhog Day*

I've never talked to anybody before. I just kept everything in. Aye on you go, just let it pass by. You feel down all the time, depressed. Now, this last couple of months I've been alright because I've been talking more. At first I wouldn't dae it 'cause, before he was no well, I had problems myself: my hearing, 'cause I can't hear in my right ear, I've lost eighty, ninety per cent. In truth, I've had my own personal loss and then my uncle died, and then my wee sister turned no well as well. So everything has kind of built up. I was down at my doctors for anti-depressants because I was really depressed masel.

I should have spoke out a long time ago, I've got a lot of things on my back. My kids changed a lot. When I see them getting nothing done for them, that's when it really hits you. Truthfully that's it, it's the children you've got to think of, not yourself. It's not just my family, it's the other people and the other kids around here. Especially the people who, as a carer, arenae getting the time to dae their own thing. I see it everywhere and I seen it when I was seventeen-year-old with ma stepmum's mother and her son. The way they were treated, it was appalling, really appalling. They said to her he would only live till he was ten but the laddie lived till he was sixteen-year-old. He had a spine condition and he couldn't walk and he couldn't do nothing. He was in pain 24/7. He had that bone eating disease, it ate all the bone tissue, the calcium in your bones, eventually his heart stopped. I seen his mum and what she should have got was emotional support, she never got anything like that. The wee boy never got anything what he should be getting like his wheelchair access and his house, because she had to carry him herself, up and doon the stairs of the house. She was sixty-year-old and she had a wee boy to look after and she wasn't well herself. It shouldn't be like that and they should be getting everything that they should be. It doesn't matter who the person is. If people can't do

Ledaig Site, Argyll

it, let them have it. She can't do it, she can't even get a passport because she can't sign her name. It's not just my culture, everybody should have a right.

I had my kids and that's what changed me, my kids. Everything's kind of changed in that way. I seen the way my mum was years ago as well, she was a hard woman like myself, she was a hard woman. She was only totie right enough but she had strength, it was unbelievable but she wouldnae wait for any man. If she wanted anything she went and done it herself. That was the kind of woman she was. She used to tell me, "If you like it, do it. That's it, don't wait just do it." That's the kind of person she was. My mum wouldn't let me get let down when I was younger, so why should I do that to them. I want someone to tell me where to go, where I can get the kind of things I should be getting for the kids. Things for kids, for the kids. Truthfully if you want to take your kids, it is going to cost you money. I could do with taking my kids and it isn't going to cost money. You're having a good time, you come back and that lets you relax and you'll find the kids enjoy themselves. But I think everything is to do with money now, everything is money. Money, money, money and I just don't have it.

Some weeks I can't afford to go and get the gas. That's how bad it is because it's £38 for a wee half bottle and I have to buy two of them every fortnight. I cannae keep that going, keep my lecy going, keep the shopping going. Sometimes I put diesel in the car to get us about. If not I have to get buses to put my kids up to school every day. That's five pound a day just to do that. I cannae keep it up; I don't get a lot of money. If he was able to work he'd be doing the right thing, exactly. But he's no able to do it. He's had surgery in his knees. He's in pain all the time, all the time. He's been like this now for the last five year. They told him straight they can't do nothing. It's pain in the morning, pain at night, pain before he gets up. But that's the way it is every day.

We got away for eight weeks, in the summer we got funding for respite, a first for us, the kids enjoyed it because they were doing things every day. So it was good for them. We went to a massive beach, pure white sand it went on forever more. We got three big stones, you took a bit off, one for wealth, peace and love. So I've got them lying there, those wee bits of stones. And then the old man came in with the horses.

Libby Brown

The weans loved that, they really, really did like that with the horses. My Mary, she started, she wanted a horse and the man came o'er, "Would yous like tae buy it?" "No, nowhere to put it. Too much upkeep." So my father-in-law he got one. It's pure black. It's a beautiful horse but it wisnae broken in, so they were feeding it Hobnobs through the window. Feeding it Hobnobs through the window, they loved that.

It was peaceful and quiet and no worries. There was no likes of councils, appointments, nothing just a break, away from everything. Freedom that's it, so it was quite good that way. I seen my cousins that I'd never seen since they were that size, quite small. I had to look twice to see who it was because I didn't recognise them, because the last time I seen them they were only nine and ten. So when I seen them yon day, they were married with kids. I didnae recognise them. One is away to Canada to stay. I'll no get to see her for a good while now.

Now I feel depressed, no-one comes to see me, don't go anywhere, just sit and do the same thing over and every day. I get up in the morning, put my kids to school, go and get my shopping, come back here, go to my appointment, come back again. Then I've got him to worry about. It's like *Groundhog Day*. It's no very good if you've got to do that every single day. You need to be doing some-thing different every day. But I think everybody feels like that.

I don't know about my future but I want my kids to have an education. The way I see it, you've got to have an education 'cause you don't get anywhere in life with no education. The trick was I never got no education when I was younger because my mum passed away, I was seven-years-old and it was just my dad. I was a mum to my wee brother and sister and myself. I never stayed at home. I went working with my dad every day but the other two I made sure they had an education. I was always good that way. I think it's because I'm old, I've always been old. I've always been like that, looking after the other ones.

Libby Brown

We Were Never Settled

WE were never settled so if my dad did take unwell then my mum would get him to the doctor, onto some valium or some other meds. We got moved from place to place, so there was never no place to go back to where the health people knew his condition or his medical history. My dad was admitted to hospital. One day he just walked away, he had all the money in his pocket, and he went to a bus-stop and offered it to this young man. The young man sort of knew there was something wrong, so he called the police and said, "There's a man here trying to hand me a lot of money." So the police brought him to my mum and she said, "Look you're going to have to get a doctor. You can't just arrest him." So the doctor came and assessed him and they took him up to Larbert for a few weeks. And then he got home and he was fine.

Edith

Thomas's Pickup

He has a little pickup
All shiny and red
And if I did not know better
I think he would take it to bed.

He says it's old
He says it's slow
But it will take you
Wherever you want to go.

With his name on the door
He drives it with pride
Sometimes with me
At his side.

He lets you see it
He talks from dawn till dusk
And you would not see
One speck of rust.

It is his pride and joy
It is his special toy
I know he is a man
But he thinks he's a boy.

I don't know what to do
As I am sad and blue
That pickup is number one
And I am number two.

He would not take silver
He would not take gold
As you see that little pickup
Never will be sold.

Katrina Stewart

Keepsakes

They're just things from people to remember them by. I don't get to see people so much 'cause so many are in houses now. These are all things people have given me. Years ago if boys and girls were together, the girls would give the boy a hairband or bobble and he would put it on the gear stick or mirror in the motor – that was supposed to be their cement as boyfriend and girlfriend.

Corrina

Walks And Steps Through Life

My mother's been through so many walks and steps through life. It's like a great journey. She had nine of us and went oot hawking, bare begging, working in fields, thinning neeps, picking tatties, picking berries, making flowers, selling flowers, everything; you mention it she did it. I seen us with nothing, I mean nothing even to eat, and her going out, what they called bare begging at that time, and coming home with food and clothes. This wisnae hawking, hawking was like if she was selling lace or clothes pegs or as we called it swag. But bare begging meant going with her hands in her pockets with nothing to offer except her voice and her stories. She was amazing.

She would never lie, she was direct, upfront, truthful. And she always told the truth because she used to read the crystal ball and dae horoscopes and she would always tell the people the truth of what she thought because she could read people like a book. And I remember one woman came to her and gave

Kathy's family in front of their horse-drawn wagon

her a hundred pound note because what she told her in her horoscope came true. And she says, "I owe my whole happiness to you," and she says, "Take that," and she opened her hand, then she went away and it was a hundred pound.

Kathy's mother in Ullapool

My dad travelled a lot throughout England, followed all the work. Me, I started working when I was about five, I started picking tatties up at Crieff. I had a half bit, my brothers had a half bit and one of my sisters and my mum had a full bit. She had to help me and my brothers. She was an amazing woman, I never knew someone like her and no just because she was my mum, she was my best friend as well. After my dad died she started taking illnesses, her kidneys failed, she was on dialysis and nearly died a couple of times. Nearly died having a couple of her kids too. She just had a hard old life but was a strong woman. She always said she'd come from the Indians. Her favourite man in the whole world was Geronimo.

My dad died in 1982 so it was just about a year after that she started going down hill after she came back from Canada. It was basically her kidneys because at twenty-one she was diagnosed with pernicious anaemia for which she had to get statin injections for the rest of her life, so she got them every month on the button. Then her kidneys went and then she had a heart attack. She was took to Edinburgh and after she recovered from her kidneys eventually, she was never the same. This was right on from 82 to

87, 88 quite a long time, and over that period of years she was quite ill.

My wee brother by then had turned eighteen and had gone away with the girl he was choosing as his wife. They had a few years together and then he went back to live with mum and shortly after that he started taking mentally ill which was very stressful for her. With my brother too I was his carer for about five year wi' my mother 'cause she started to get too frail. That was a lot of pressure because the more she got stressed with his care, then I was getting more wi' her care.

There was times I used to go in to help her cook dinner and do stuff she wisnae able to do any more and she'd be sitting crying that my brother had hit her. But she hid it until I found out for myself one day. I was furious but there was nothing I could do because he wisnae well and the doctors and nurses from that point took over my wee brother, but he was still allowed to live at home. Basically she was his cook, cleaner and loved him. No matter what he did, she loved him. Sometimes I'd go in to take care of her and you'd end up taking care of the both of them. We always called her mammy and it was so hard for me sometimes just not to take it out on him and I found it very difficult at times no to say something to him because you loved him tae and he used to sit and he used to cry and ask me for help. And mammy used to say, "Just give him a cuddle, he'll be alright."

Even when they gave him electric shock treatment when they took him to a locked unit, I think they misinterpreted it because he was a Traveller. We had different ways and they didnae know how to handle that. The people didnae know enough about Travellers. He was wanting ootside and telling stories. That's what Travellers do, and they just thought it was mentalness and it wisnae looked at right.

How do you make people understand that he was used to being ootside all the time, no used to being contained especially when he was put in a padded cell one time. He was telling them, "I'm going to get myself a trailer and a new van and then I'm off." They were taking it that he was literally going to run away from the hospital and it was being mis-interpreted all the time.

It was hard because I watched her in a lot of pain sometimes. Even me helping her bathe, her dignity was getting hurt 'cause she would try and shy away even from me. It was just seeing that woman with that stamina took doon to that level. You know you had to help her into the bathroom, you had to help her wash, help her dress and you've got a mentally-ill brother lying in the next room. Sometimes you'd just be finished with her and you'd go next door and he'd be sitting crying and wanting help.

I used to work all day and come back, see to my four kids and my man and then I used to go round and start at my mum's. Some nights I'd get finished at half eleven then I'd go hame, iron the school claes and then

Kathy and her mum in Dunkeld, 1990s

I'd get up at six and away to work. I wanted to gie my children schooling because I had never been to school. This went on for like nine, ten year. My marriage split up. Along wi' other things, wi' no being there, my brother being the way he wis sometimes. I just thought I was going to explode at one point.

At one point we had a home-help, which my mother hated. She hated it because they couldnae clean right, according to her, couldnae cook right and see they meals they took into her, they left her sick because she liked pot roasts and pots of soup and stews. "Ken the meat they make," she used to say, "Kathy it's going to kill me. I'm no gaunie di wi' illness, I'm gaunie di' wi' this." I says, "Look mammy they have to come and gie you something to eat during the day when I'm no here." I felt like I was letting her doon. So when I was getting back, I felt I had this pressure to hurry up and go aroon' and get things done for them. Sometimes you'd find yourself making pots of meat at night, so they could have something for lunch during the day and a wee drop tea if I wisnae back in time, because sometimes I had to work late as well, like overtime.

I wouldnae change it for the world but I felt there was an awful lot of pressure. Sometimes I would just cry my eyes oot, but you would always try and hide it. I'm good at that now because I've been through that much that I can just hide things, but at one point I went on anti-depressants and valium just to keep myself standing. I think if I had known what I know now I could have asked for mair help. I could have got roon it a lot better if I had asked for things. Caring's not put across enough to us sort. We can care for ourselves and others around us, like my mammy there, but there's probably a lot more I could have done for her if I had known a lot more.

This is one feeling I don't know if I want to share or no. See when she died, I thought if God's got her she's free. She believed very much in God and always used to say, "Where's your stamina? God's wi' us." I used to say, "Is God going tae fill us the night?" "He will!" I think he was her second man half the time. Oh I miss her yet!

Kathy McGuigan

If I Were A Bird

If I were a bird
I would fly so high
We would touch the moon, stars and sky
I would fly over mountains
Tall and small
I would watch the sea rise and fall
I would nest in a tree
That touched the sky
I would wave at the others that passed me by
I would sit on a steeple
And watch all the people
I would whistle and sing
And do everything
The places I would go
The things I would see
If I were a bird I'd be free

Katrina Stewart

Fishing Rod

The thing that is significant about this is that my grandfather let me fly-fish with this rod when I was eight, aye eight-year-old. I always went fishing with my grandad up at Crieff and by Glen Lyon. He loved his fly-fishing.

Tom

I Am A Gypsy

I was thirteen when we moved up to Oban, not long out of primary school. Well my dad wanted to be back up here because here is where he's from. We stayed on the site there and we did get a lot of stick when we first came up here. They'd say, "Just go back to where you come from," and, "What yous doing here?" and "Yous are no welcome here." But then as years went on, and as my sister and brother went to school here, we got to know the locals and they're kind of used to us being here now. We're just part of the community basically; that's the whole thing, we are part of the community, staying out at the site.

I moved off the site and into Oban with my partner, he's a country man, a non-Traveller. We left Oban and went to Falkirk and had my wee boy, he's six now. Aye, after I had my wee boy, Kieran, we moved back up here, to the site first, then got a house in Oban.

I have had a lot of discrimination from the police here. They never really bothered me out at the site, and they don't any more now that I'm out at the site again. It was just when I was in Oban here that they bothered me. They would just come lift me for no reason, say suspicion for something, into the cells, I'd lie the weekend and then get oot on the Monday. But we got a lot of discrimination. Then through no fault of theirs – my own fault – I jumped in a car drunk and I got done for drunk-driving and I got eighteen months and a four-and-a-half-year driving ban.

I met quite a few lassies in the jail that would talk to me, bits of broken Cant, you know what I mean, and then as soon as a crowd came around them, that would all drop and nothing more would be mentioned about Travellers. I am not like that. Oh no way! You're a Traveller standing there and denying it to everybody else. Do you know what I mean? As soon as I went in I was like, "I am Charlene MacDonald and I am a Gypsy." I told them straight up and then they all found that interesting and they were all, "That would be a good lifestyle," and asked me questions about

Charlene MacDonald and Kieran

it. Aye I didn't get much bother because I was, "Here's who I am and I am doing a sentence just the same as the rest of you."

When I was on remand Kieran's dad had him doon every weekend but when I was in the jail he only brought him down once because he pished the bed after the visit, so I said, "Don't bring him back doon." That broke my heart. Oh my God, it was heart-breaking, it was really soul-destroying. It's the hardest thing I've ever done in my life being away from Kieran that long.

In prison I asked my personal officer about getting tagged to the site. She said, "I really don't know how that would work."

I said, "But I've heard of it, other Travellers have got it done." She was expecting me to get a knock-back.

The man who worked with the tags came doon into the cells and he asked, "Is that a permanent address you are going to?"

I said, "I've lived there for years."

Then he came back and said, "You've been granted your tag." Aye there was a lot of officers there that thought that was really unusual.

They were asking, "How does it work 'cause your toilet's outside?" and they were asking, "How far a radius you would get?"

I said, "I don't know, I'm new to this too."

I've had a bit of help. I was seeing a Community Psychiatric Nurse (CPN), I was seeing her for about a year and then I was seeing an addictions worker for a year as well but mainly my CPN – she was a really big help. But it's my

Ledaig Site, Argyll

mum, she's been absolutely fantastic! I wrote a poem for her when I was inside, how I'd always let her down but she'd always been there for me whatever, she's so strong.

Kieran's with his dad now, he's got him full-time, he's been absolutely fantastic with Kieran because I really messed up before I went to jail. I was heavy on drink, really messed up. He could have just taken Kieran like that and I couldnae have done

a thing aboot it. I couldnae ask for any better than he's been with Kieran. Now I pick him up from school and get the five o'clock bus back and then at the weekend he comes oot to the site and stays with me all weekend.

My plan is to go to college, I'm going to try and get into a counselling course. So I'm just hoping that goes ahead. It's something I've always wanted to do, but see when I was in prison that last time, there was this man who came in. He had done quite a long time in jail and he was a recovering heroin addict, but he was five-year clean and he was working as a counsellor in the prison. I'd wanted to do it way before I seen that. But see when I seen that, I said there is hope yet because he had quite a criminal record; he was telling me about things that he had done. Aye he had quite a lengthy criminal record, same as myself, and I thought aye that's something I want to do.

Charlene MacDonald

Xbox
I love my Xbox. It's first-class. I save all my money so I can buy a new game.

Sandy

Clappy Doos - Better Than The Ritz

I am a granny to forty-one, a great-granny to forty-two and the branch is still spreading on the tree. Weans were never a bother to me, if I put on a pot, they each got. I reared mine up on my own and went out grafting every day with my basket.

This photo was taken in Arrochar; that being the month of July they'd be heading to Glencoe. That's me in my mammy's arms; I'm about nine-months-old. I was born in a bow camp like this on the bonny banks of Loch Lomond right at the top end. There's

a wee wood and my auntie Mary collected brackens off the hillside for mammy's labour bed. Many years later, auntie Mary lived with me and I cared for her until she died.

Mammy had a difficult birth with me, only seven month gone; when I did come into the world they thought I was dead, rolled me in a sheet and put me at mammy's feet. But the grannies wanted to see me, me being the first grandwean on each side. They unwrapped the sheet and seen a pulse on me. I was known as the 'seven person', born at seven months on the twenty-seventh of the seventh month of 1937. I was always petted, known as wee Isa. My mother went on to have another ten, all outside, never in a hospital, and I delivered the last one.

This is granny Belle on Pitlochry bridge. She always had a soft spot for me, her namesake. It's a right tourist spot and they'd stand and sell white heather, anything for a shilling as long as it was honest. I mind she liked her earrings and wee fancy shoes; she lived

into her nineties you know. I remember as a lassie going up the Rest and Be Thankful with a wagon. We'd an old white horse called Nelly but my daddy believed we'd also to push the back of the wagon. They must've been tarring the road 'cause I remember digging our toes into the soft tar as we pushed. We stopped at the wee loch and there were tourists fishing; the salmon were dancing about. The man passed the fish to my daddy. We went on to Inveraray, there'd been a freak storm and we got clappy doos (like big mussels) on the shore. My mammy had been selling baskets, got a bit ham and fried up the bacon and clappy doos in oatmeal on an open fire, along with the salmon. What a supper we had that night; you couldn't have got better at the Ritz.

This is uncle Anthony. He was in the two world wars. In the first one he was a despatch rider and lost his leg. I mind when I was wee him showing us his tin leg. Him, uncle Jimmy and uncle Robert

were taken off my granny and granda for the schooling: in those days you'd to do two hundred and two attendances or you got taken to a home and they weren't allowed to see them those days. When they turned sixteen they all went to the army. Uncle Jimmy he went to India for sixteen years and could speak Punjabi. Uncle Robert, he went down at Scapa Flow.

My uncle Anthony and the nurse who

tended him fell in love, they married and went on to have eight weans. He was my auntie Mary's wee brother, so I found him and got them back together after no seeing each other for near on forty years. He stayed all his days in England, in Dover, but his last request was for his ashes to come back to Scotland. You know the Pass of Glencoe, that's where me and my son took him; I think he'd have liked that.

My auntie Mary, or Peedy Poddy, that was her nickname, she came to us thirty-two years ago. After her husband died, I got her down to stay with me. I was in my forties and she was in her fifties and we stayed over twenty-five years together. She was tiny but she always liked a dram, no water in it mind. It was the smoker's disease that took her in the end. Me, I don't take medication for nothing – if I go, then I go. That's what I say.

Now I'm settled but I prefer to be in the trailer. I get awfy restless, always away gallivanting. You can hear the rain breaking on the roof of a trailer; if you are blue before, then when you're away in the trailer you're as happy as a lark. For me it's like therapy. Even now, I still get itchy feet, still a rolling stone – nature is always there, I'm proud of what I am. Mind I'm no very Travellerfied in this photo.

Isa Johnstone

I've Heard People Say

I've heard people that stay in hooses say, "Stay away from that caravan site." Not knowing that I'm a Traveller and I'm running aboot with their boy and they've just turned roond said to their boy's baby brother, "Stay away from up that road 'cause that's where those Gypsies stay and they'll take you and we'll never see you again" – I'm sitting back thinking they dinnae know I'm a Traveller: if only they knew I was running aboot with their oldest son and I'm a Traveller and they've just said that. I don't know what gets us that persona; I don't know why people think that about us but it's horrible when you hear it first-hand.

Winky

Travelling

I don't have a postcode
Nowhere to call home
I am a Traveller you see
I just like to roam.

Some roads are long, some are short
I know this well as I have travelled all
For an hour or two or maybe a day
But I would not have it any other way.

The places I go, the people I meet
Some are nice, some are bittersweet
Where I travel I do not know
But I will travel through rain, sleet and snow.

I've travelled south
I've travelled north
Maybe someday east or west
And may I say, I travel with the best.

Katrina Stewart

Mobile Phone

There could be somebody hundreds of miles away and without my Blackberry there would be no communication, imagine? I'd die without it. It's got to be a Blackberry for BBM and you can ping anyone, anywhere.

Mary

A Pebble In A Pond

My name's Edith Townsley, I've growed up on the road my whole life. I've never lived in a house. I don't consider myself a carer but it's like throwing a pebble in a pond when somebody's unwell. The ripples go on way past the person who's unwell and way past the one who's taking most care of them; it affects a lot more than one person.

Probably what makes me the person I am today is that I've lived through so much anguish, call it pain, and you get through it and it makes you a more understanding person towards somebody else's problems or feelings.

I've been aware of mental heath since I was a child because my dad had some minor mental health issues. So I grew up aware of mental health and the changes in a person when they become unwell. You know they take bouts. My mum would just say, "Your dad's not well." So you were always aware to keep the noise down, and then when you get older, then you pick up for yourself the difference – in their appearance, the look on their face, or their actions change.

My dad died when I was fourteen; my mum was in hospital at that time so I had to tend my dad for seven weeks – to a fourteen-year-old that's a long time. And I had my wee baby brother to look after and feed. Sometimes you could see him taking unwell and getting worse but at that age I didn't have the sense to walk into the town and say, "I need help."

My older brother Luke was there. So I told him dad's taken awfy no well to the extent that I couldnae get to the kitchen to make my wee brother anything to eat. He'd hear the pots and he'd be, "Stop that! Sit down!" and we went back to bed. I remember, again, my brother Luke, he opened the trailer door and he crept in along the floor on his hands and knees, pulled the door behind him on the old-fashioned Buccaneer-type caravan, sneaked up, put his hand up, caught mine and just stayed there. I gave him blankets and that's what he did, just held my hand till morning and then I fell asleep knowing that he was there.

Luke has always been, the way I see it, me and my wee brother's carer. Luke was always there for me. He did it all the way through the years and never asked for nothing. Recently I thought I was having a minor breakdown and he came up for two days, seen me through it. Just held me, cuddled me. You know he's fifty odds and he's still here for me.

My dad died in the trailer, he was dressed in the trailer and taken away from there to Rattray cemetery. I remember when we were paying our last respects and everybody was going in and giving my dad a kiss on the brow and my wee brother wouldn't do it and he didn't shed a tear. He never did to this day. He was eleven, but the scars remain. So when he was no well himself, I felt it was just history repeating itself. I've always been going to mental hospitals. You think, when's it going to end?

In the Traveller community mental health's not talked about outside your home. What's under your roof is family stuff, you go out and play with the other kids and nothing is mentioned. So you have to deal with it inside. I'm forty-four now and it doesn't leave you. I suppose what me and my brother went through with my dad has stemmed onto him. Well, I would say, contributed at least to his condition. You weren't took for counselling, it wasn't talked about. You just dealt with it.

So when he took unwell he was still living with my mother, although she wasn't fit to care for him but she did. They couldn't get benefits, she tried once and she was, how did they put it, she was physically too unfit to be a carer, to care after somebody with his condition and he was too unfit, mentally unfit, to be her carer.

At first he lay for nine days in mother's house without eating, drinking or getting up. So she thought right it's time to phone.

Edith's brother in his trailer

said, "I think we'll have to get him up to hospital for a while – just to get him sorted out." So the ambulance came and he just walked into it. He'd got to the point where he needed hospitalisation.

We went up the next day. After the meds wore off he was roaring and shouting, "There is nothing wrong with me why am I here?" So it took him a long time, he was stubborn. You know he'd been out and in, he'd spent eighteen months in Carstairs as well. He was transferred to Carstairs through an incident, he got aggravated or something.

You should try and go visiting in that hospital. I used to take my kids up with me. He was sensible enough to say, "Please don't take the girls up in here!" So then I got somebody to come with me and sit in the car with the kids. It's like a terrible, terrible place to go. The regime that you've got to go through before you even get in to see somebody is unbelievable. You've got to get a photo. You've got to get a name tag sent

She phoned the GP, he came out and just basically asked his name and if he knew if it was night or day. Obviously he didn't. He

out to you processed. Then you go through a door and into an office, give your name, then you sit. Then a door buzzes that'll open, closes behind you. Then you've got a thing like the airport security, everything comes out, you get scanned: obviously you're not allowed to take certain things into Carstairs. Then another door opens and you go through and you pick up your stuff. Then you go outside and you stand and this bus comes.

Carstairs is not just one big hospital: when you look up on the hill it's like a village with all different units. But down in the car-park, in the main reception you're out on the pavement. The bus comes. The bus fills up. The two gates open. The bus goes through. The bus stops. The gate closes behind the bus. There's another gate in front of the bus, but the one in front of the bus doesn't open till the gate behind closes. Then the bus takes you up to whatever unit you're visiting and it's a terrible place to go visit. So he was there

for a wee while and then we got him back to the local hospital and believe it or not I think my mam appreciated the time he was there because the doctors at Carstairs actually sorted him oot. When he went to Carstairs they diagnosed him as schizophrenic so they put him on the correct medication and he's fine and he talks.

About two year ago and four months is the last time I seen my wee brother because he decided, "Well what's the point of seeing anybody because nobody is going to be able to help me anyway. They can't get me out of here." So he just sort of gave up on his family. It doesnae only hurt him, it hurts me. I says, "He can turn round and say he wants no visitors and you abide by that because it's his choice." But I says, "I put it to you that it's not his choice to be in here, it's not his choice to be locked up behind that door all the time. You are taking that choice away from him but you're allowing him different choices." Not only that, but if you phone up the ward they give you no information without his permission. Even general stuff like how is he on a daily basis, what does he do, does he go into the games room, has he lost weight, has he gained weight? Just like, "How are you doing? Are you okay?" Stuff like that. You find out nothing.

My life was circled round every Sunday. No matter where I was in the country I would go to the hospital on a Sunday, whether I had to bus it, train it, walk it, or get a lift. You know that was my time with him. So when he stopped seeing me my whole life had to change as well. I've seen me go to the door and say, "I know he doesnae want to see me but please get him to give me the thumbs up at the windae or something. I just need to see his face." I'd go from that hospital and I'd have to park somewhere and just break down. But then I'd say to myself, "I've seen him and he's gied me the thumbs up." I miss actually seeing his face, you know what I mean.

Edith Townsley

The Pain Of Losing My Father

In my heart there is a pain
Knowing I'll never see your face again
As I stand here to say goodbye
I promised myself I would not cry
But that's so hard to do
So forgive me dad if you see a tear or two
As I stand here by your side
With my heart filled with love and pride
I know I have to let you go
But now in my heart I want you back

Katrina Stewart

Peg Basket

Survival. My mama's lifeline. Freedom. For us it was a packet o' crisps as we hiked our way hame at the end of the week. Memories flood back, it always put a smile on her face. After she was hoosed up she would look at the basket and say, "If I could …"

Kathy

She Always Wore The Gypsy Pinnies

Well I'm Betty, I'm a Gypsy/Traveller and I live on a council site. I love it here, but I haven't always been on a site. I used to travel a lot as a child, and a teenager too, visiting different camps with my family, but then I ended up staying in a house for a while, as an adult ye know. I started living in a house about five years ago, on my own.

Agh, in that house I felt so closed in and I didnae want the neighbours to know what I come off – Travelling folk you know. I was very stressed there, agitated, uncontented, that's it – uncontented. I felt very lonely there, my family didnae stay round about there – no close family anyway, no parents or brothers or that. I was always feared if family would turn up in vans or trailers in case the neighbours would find out who I was. I wisnae able to be myself at all.

I told family I couldnae get contented in the house. I tried to get on the site three years ago but the site was really full. I also didnae have money for the trailer and that in

truth, so I had to delay it. Finally, I handed in my notice on the house and here I am. I just thought, even if I dinnae get on the site I'm not staying in a house, enough's enough.

You know, coming back to this site is like another life. I slipped right into it – like a duck into water! It feels like I've never left. I'm just back to my roots, it's as simple as that. And I'm okay with visitors here. I'm not worried about that now. Truthfully, I should have done this years ago, that's my only regret.

My granny is Bella Armstrong and she was based on Bellshill site when it first opened, and I used to go over and stay with her, I think I was only about eighteen or nineteen. I hadnae towed a trailer, so I used to get my uncle or my nephews to come and tow the trailer and take us to other sites, just to let her get a wee break. So we used to go to Douglas. The man was really nice on there, and he used to let Travellers on, but a lot of the people that stayed there, the locals, didnae like Travellers at all, they just werenae for Travellers. During the day we hawked out a lot of the houses, me and her for a few hours, for a few days, met a lot of nice people. But night time I said to my granny, "I think we'll go over to that hotel and have something to eat." When we came out of the hotel we couldnae get back to the site for all young boys saying, "Gypsies and Tinkers!" and aw. We were feared that night and the door didnae lock on the trailer. Oh I really had a fear that night. They were all round about the trailer and they were all shouting. The man in the house heard them. I had to phone my uncle to tell the boys fer to come over to shift us. I think the thing is, see my granny, she liked to wear a pinny. I used to say to her, "Please take that pinny off granny." Honestly people know right away, they do. She always wore the Gypsy pinnies. She had a coat on, but they would still see the pinny under it, and she done what you call a lot of dukering, that's like

telling the fortunes. She done a lot of that, and I done it as well, I was only young but mother learnt me how to do it.

This photo here, this is mother, and she's pulling the horse and the wagon and that's her sister on the right-hand side. Mother's only seventeen there. And my auntie Bella,

she'll be fifteen. They've got their pinnies on. She's got her hair tied back, scarf on too, she had long blond hair and mother had long red hair, but they used to wear a lot of plaits, tie them back and they used to cross them over.

This picture here, this is my father, and I think he was about twenty-two in it. It was back in the '50s, he's on the left-hand side. Next to him that's his cousin, and that's his brother, that's my uncle at the back with the wee dog. And these girls here, they're all my father's nieces 'cause my father comes off eight of a family, and he had three brothers and four sisters. I don't know where this photo actually is you know, I think it's down Ayrshire 'cause that's where my father's people come from, the Galloway coast. My dad's mother was Bella Stewart. They camped down there a lot 'cause they had a lot of family down there.

Have you noticed there, my dad's got his sovereign on? Did you see that? And his muffler, dae ye see that too? He's got his muffler on, see that's what a lot of the Travellers wore years ago. See that around his neck. But not just the men, I've got photos of my granny with a muffler but she didnae always wear it on her neck, she wore it round her head. My auntie Bella too, she always wears it, every time you see her, she wears it round her neck. Violet too: one day I went out there I was quite surprised, 'cause she's like a woman. She was going to a Christian meeting or something and I said, "Oh my God." I never see that unless I see it on my aunties, but Violet had a muffler on and it was nice.

Betty Irvine

Photo Frame

It's important to me 'cause it's my twins with my only lassie. I love Crown Derby. What Traveller woman doesn't? I try to buy pieces when I can afford it.

Evelyn

It Was A Great Life

When we were travelling about from place to place we were down at Lochgilphead 'cause we were picking the whelks and on our way to Perth. When we started back, at the Dunoon road end a boy come up and smashed into us. I was trapped in the van for a couple of hours and my mother, she was on the other side and her leg was bleeding and her face was bleeding. We ended up in hospital for three months in Glasgow and my mother lost her leg from the accident and from then on things started to go wrong.

When we got out of hospital we managed to struggle from place to place, still getting on, still living in a trailer, doing our cultural thing. She was still able to go about, do her shopping, do her hawking. We did that for about twenty-five years until we had to move into a house.

For the last six-and-a-half years I was caring for my mother because she was starting to go into dementia. Even at that

David McDonald visiting his mother Catherine in hospital

stage, she could still go to the post office and do the wee routine things up to about the last two years. She was aye bad and I had to get some way of getting care. I didn't know much about the Carer Centre or anything like that. Someone put me onto it and I just walked in one day. From then onwards I started to need letters read and forms filled up because I can't read or write and my

David on the shores of Loch Etive

mother did all that for me. If it wisnae for the people at the centre I would have been completely lost.

What really put us off the road was the authorities, the police and people like that. They just got down to business, went up to higher authorities and they just stopped people from moving about from place to place, what we should have been doing, and what we should still be doing yet. That's the time that Travellers are more happy, when they're moving about, and they're more healthy. I mean they stopped all that. It's put us in a place where we are sort of prisoned off, just like open jails. My brother-in-law, he has taken it very, very serious because he cannae get to move from place to place. My sister is just down on it. It's breaking people's health. I had a spell like that, that I just wisnae too well, depressed and stuff like that. But since my mother got care I've got sort of round it. You know I've moved out of it, I'm sort of back to normal, you could say.

I went to the Scottish Parliament to try and help people to get on with their caring business and to see if they could do any better for the carers. I went to give information that was needed to bring it up to standard for people in the future. I just told them in the Parliament that they will have to pay attention to us. I felt it was a good thing to do. There's not enough Travellers getting onto the Parliament about things but it was a good opportunity and if I had to go back I would.

David McDonald

Sovereign

This is what women wore years ago, the sovereign. My gran would have worn it. They always wore full sovereigns or half sovereigns. They used to have them mounted or bent: they'd have earrings or rings or necklaces. The day it's not something lassies would be interested in. Then, they wore jewellery, jewellery – lots of it, but not now.

Violet

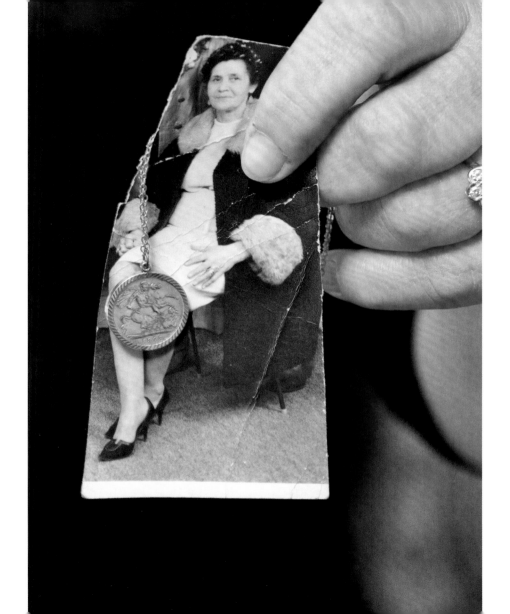

Getting Through It

My mam's got dementia. She is eighty-two years of age and it would be different if she was a fit eighty-two but she's not and she's incapable of doing anything for herself and somebody has to be with her 24/7. Even when you're asleep she's awake and she's wandering about and she's coming in putting her hands on you and waking you. Then when she takes sick, she loses all her memory and her balance goes and she thinks there's people in the room coming down on top of her. I take it on because she's my mother and she raised me and like why should I put her into a home?

Then last December I found out what's been causing my two kids to be so sick. I was raised up with me sister and I used to help her babysit her three children and all of them had cystic fibrosis (CF). So I knew an awful lot about CF, an awful lot. At two weeks and four days my eldest son, Bobby, had all the symptoms of CF. He had the salt on his skin, an ongoing chest infection, a loss of weight and breathing problems. I told the doctors he had symptoms of CF but he wasn't diagnosed They said it was just asthma. It took fourteen years to get the correct diagnosis as CF and now my daughter, Precious, has it too. They told me they both had asthma for all those years.

At the end of last year all five of my children had to be tested and I was waiting twenty days. Two of them came back that they had it. The way I was the day I found out about them, I had to be sedated – that's how bad I took it.

A massive problem is that the social workers treated me so bad. We explained I had a problem with reading and writing, that I couldn't hardly understand a lot of the big words they were coming out with. As far as I am concerned they treated me so bad because they knew I couldn't read or write, they knew I was a Traveller and they just said she can't get nothing done to us and she doesn't have a clue. But they are mistaken. I am a human being and I am a person. The only help I got from social

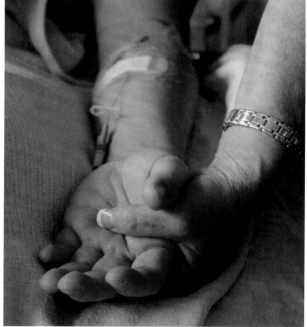

Martina comforts her son as he undergoes more tests

work was for diesel money for all the travel I was doing to hospital. It was £20 and she made me break out crying, that woman did. At a time like this nobody should be treated like that no matter whether they are Gypsies or not. I wouldn't treat another person like that. They made me feel so guilty.

They should have at least showed me a bit of support over Christmas, which can be a very emotional time for anybody, never mind somebody going through that. After watching my husband die nine years before and five days before Christmas, it was horrible watching two kids getting taken away and operations done to their lungs and pipes and drips and everything coming out of them.

I felt really bad that I had to get social workers involved in my life because I did it on my own for nine years. I did it nine year and I didn't have social workers and I felt really good about it, do you know what I mean. It gives me a sense of pride to say, "Tina you reared these children on your own, by you and the power of God, and you never needed help. You did get family tax credit and you did get income support, but you never had social workers involved. You never had police. You never had other Travellers to help you. You did it on your own." It made me feel good, made me feel that one day the children would look around and say, "My mother did it on her own." It gave me a bit of security to know that I did do that.

When the social workers got involved and the children got sick, the social workers put me down an awful lot, and it made me feel I wasn't good enough for the children, and I wasn't treating the children good. The first time I seen the social worker she said, "That's what we're here for Martina. We're here to help you. We're here to give you the support." Then she went out and when she came back she was a total different person and she said, "The most that we have is £20. There's a limit on who we give money to." Who's entitled to it, does it go by your skin?

Just now with me having the two kids in hospital and my mum living with me, I'm not rightly sure if she's going to keep on living with me, 'cause for the days that I'm back in the hospital it means that mum's at home with my oldest daughter. It's a lot for a seventeen-year-old, because it's an awful lot to feed somebody and wash them three to four times a day, plus the stress of her brother and sister in the hospital. She's not coping very well just now and I can see it. She'll say, "I don't want it, mammy," and, "I can't believe it how you've so many things to do with old mammy." That's what they call her, they don't call her granny they call her old mammy 'cause she's the older mammy. I think she wanted to put her hands around me and just cry.

You find out how hard it is to struggle but you still get through it. You have to keep on walking but you will fall down and probably get a cut but you have to get yourself back up again – that's all I've been going through.

The children is a support to me, they are my strength and my oxygen. If my oxygen is low at ninety-five they can just come on and give me the five extra. They're like when you get a punctured wheel, then you get a new one and you're back to normal again. The kids is like the fixer that make me come back and everything is normal again, thank God, and we've always been together.

Martina Doherty

Football Strips

When I was growing up I always used to play a football game, me and my brother, and there was a player Thierry Henry, and I liked him best. He used to play for Arsenal and I like the colour of the top. My brother supported Arsenal too.

James

More Than Just Words

ART is therapeutic, like a release mechanism from the pressures of life. Life is fraught with difficulties for Gypsy/Travellers; art can be used to channel all that negativity in a positive way. It helps restore a sense of mental wellbeing and boosts self-esteem.

I do it as a means of social commentary, using it as a tool, as indictment for mistreatment. I like to do the Traveller work rough around the edges because life is rough around the edges. It is like writing a book, you use your own experiences, you can use it to enlighten people. It's a way of keeping alive the memories. It makes you have a rosy glow but it's also sad.

Art can touch people more than words. You look at a scene and you can feel the emotion. I feel it can be used positively to break down prejudice. You can use art as a direction, you can carry people. For me, the arts in their entirety are a form of community engagement.

Gypsy/Travellers have always produced arts, so I am carrying on that tradition and when I am painting I feel good. It relieves some of the pressure from my life.

When I do my art, no-one can control me. They can't alter it in any way ... I'm beyond political control, that's where I'm taking back power.

Shamus McPhee

Paradise Lost.
Oil on canvas 2003

Big Chill at Bobbin Mill.
Oil on board 2003

Los Desaparecidos.
Oil on board 2003

Jeanie

For the last three years I've been a carer for my sister-in-law, Jeanie. I took her in 'cause she had no-one and she was wandering in the town. She's really forgetful and she's got difficulty doing things, so she needs help every day. They say I am the appointee for her and I do do a lot. I dinnae stop, I really dinnae stop. The only time I stop is when I go to my bed.

On this pitch, twice the council tried to evict me because I wouldnae put Jeanie out of her caravan, but she had nowhere to go. Then they agreed to put her round the back, in the field behind my pitch and put a big fence round and blocked her in. I don't know why they did that. They put a big giant fence up, so the only way Jeanie could get through was through that wee gap there between the chalet and the toilet. It was supposed to be temporary but she was round there for well over a year and you should have seen the mess she was living in. Walking back and forward there, it was just gutters and mud. They were supposed to go back and build her a step and put slabs down for her because Jeanie's off-balance. They never done any of that. I had to get, ken like, boards and put them down for her trying to walk on. It was an awful mess she was living in, so I said she's not living another winter round there.

It's mental health she's got. She doesnae come out. She doesnae come out by herself at all. I do her cooking and her washing and do things like that for her. I try my best to take her away in the car sometimes but she just refuses to come out of the caravan. She just likes sitting in her own space. She doesn't like people around her because she's not used to it. She just likes her own caravan with her own TV, her own heater and that. That's just the way she is.

My daughter helps her as well – Megan, and all the kids really, they come round and speak to her. Nobody official comes near her. They just moan because she's still staying here. I had the council phoning me last week because of it, because she wasn't in the chalet. So I told them, "You phone the social work because they were the ones that wanted her to get the chalet and were supposed to help her. She's just coming up three years she's been here and she's had five social workers." They just keep on swapping, they get moved to different posts and new ones come. She just gets to ken one and they're taken away, then somebody new comes and they dinnae ken anything about her. She calls them the social for her money. That's what she thinks it is, if they don't come, then they'll stop her money.

Before this new man came, there was a man before that and he came round the back. Jean was still round the back when he came, and he just said that he wanted Jean in a house – like one of those special houses for people like Jeanie. I tried to tell them, "Jean's a Traveller and she's not just going to go into a house," especially when

Maggie Townsley visits Jeanie in her caravan

the doctor said she can't go and live away in the town because she wanders when she's in the town. When she came here she stopped wandering. She's happy here, she likes it, she really likes it. She's never wandered since she came here. You see years ago her gran used to stay oot here, she stayed round the corner before her mum died and I think it's a

comfort for her.

They blamed me for taking her in, but she never had nowhere else to go. I wanted her to come in with me, in my chalet, but Jeanie feels as if she can't stay beside heaps of people, so that's the reason we got a wee caravan for her to stay in. She was really happy until the warden seen her going oot and in the caravan, and that's where it all started. It is a caravan site, ken, but we're not allowed to stay in a caravan!

I had hassle after hassle from the council because they have an issue with 'doubling up'. See you're allowed to have a caravan sitting on your pitch but you're no allowed to stay in it because of health and safety or something. It's silly, aye! And it wasn't health and safety putting her round there in gutters?

I just wish they would come here, get to know us, listen and then help Jeanie, not just think they know what's best. They have meetings, housing and social work, they say things will happen but they don't. That's hard for Jeanie and for me – it's been really, really hard. It's like they talk about me and Jeanie. I find it hard to go to the meetings now 'cause I get upset, and angry sometimes too, they just don't listen – it's like I don't exist.

I do get tired sometimes. There's days Jeanie can be a handful and then sometimes I think I don't spend enough time with my own kids because I'm here so much and they're saying to me, "Why are you always away?" But it's no my fault because I've got things to dae for Jeanie. It is hard sometimes.

Maggie Townsley

I Smile

I stand
looking in the mirror
I can't believe the person looking
back is really me
no more shadows under my eyes,
fae crying in the middle of the night,
hair no longer greasy, but shining bright
so I smile real wide.
Time to go off to work
can't be late
a lot of folk are depending on me to take care of them.
For they're old and get confused, not their fault.
Like it's not my fault I was born a Traveller
and lived a different culture.

Lizzie Johnstone

Freshwater Pearls In Baby Oil

It is five hundred years of Traveller history, that is. It is illegal now, been destroyed by those who don't respect the water. My daddy fished for pearls in the River Spey and his grandparents before him – it was a hobby more than anything else in the summer. Once my daddy took a pearl to the jewellers in Perth, but they offered him pennies, so he went to the big jewellers on George Street in Edinburgh. He kept it in a wee velvet pouch and when he showed it, a whole heap of suits came about him and one wanted to write out a cheque there and then. To us it was a lot but now I know they ripped us off. It was the luck of the draw if you got a good one and all us bairns loved it.

John

Crème De La Crème

That's my grandfather [in the middle of the back row], that's the crème de la crème there, top notch pipers of the day then. He was in the Atholl Highlanders, that was taken in 1898 at the end of the Games. They'd have a gathering that's in Dunoon, the ones that have been first at the Games – you know all the good ones, the first, first, first, first; they'd all get together and pick the champion. And grandad won a gold medal.

And I'll tell you another thing; have you ever heard the one about the ball, the big ball at Blair Castle? But at the ball, they were all sitting at dinner and grandad, he was the piper. But he was passing when they were dancing and this lady, I suppose she'd a ballgown on, and she let off and my grandfather took the blame! He said, "Oh I beg your pardon." And my father told us that story umpteen times. And do you know what she did when she got him on the quiet? She slipped a £5 note in his hand. I'll bet that was a lot of money in those days, and she thanked him very, very much for taking the blame for her letting off! Imagine?

Patsy

BACK ROW (left to right)—Pipe-Corporal William Ross (2nd Scots Guards), Pipe-Major J. MacDougall-Gillies (Glasgow), D. C. Mather (Loch Carron), John Stewart (Dunkeld), Peter Wilkie (Dunkeld), Pipe-Major A. Matheson (Royal Scots), Gavin MacDougall (Aberfeldy).

FRONT ROW (left to right)—Angus MacRae (Callander), John MacColl (Oban), Pipe-Major John Cameron (2nd later 3rd Camerons), J. A. Center (Edinburgh), George Taylor (Instructor, Royal Caledonian School, London), G. S. McLennan (later Pipe-Major, Gordon Highlanders).

Bank Card

The bank card is my independence – it's something that naebody could take. That is something I gained myself. It is a very new thing to Travelling People, women in particular, because men have always been the head of the family and what he says goes and what income is generated is through him. To me, I've brought my children up to be independent to go into their own pocket and spend money as they please and not to have to answer for.

Rose

Where's The Young Ones To Go?

I'm Margaret, a Scottish Gypsy/Traveller, born in Aberdeen, travelled all my life in tents and trailers, and now live on a council site in Perth. That's me and my sisters when we were bairns. I'm the one with the bow on the left.

I feel I've been isolated all my life and it can be hard for Travellers to speak out. Mental health, caring, even now I know Travellers wouldnae really speak about these things to strangers. I wouldnae anyway – it would be a personal thing to me. I'm sixty-three now and maybe I've got different views. I don't know, you might get different views from the younger Travellers. It just was a taboo subject, if you ken my meaning: Travellers didnae like to talk about children that had a mental deficiency sort of thing.

My uncle he used to stay with my grandfather but he had a child's brain. I mind he was even younger than me when I was ten. He had two favourite songs; he used to sing them like he had rehearsed them, 'Robin Hood, Robin Hood riding through the glen' and, 'Come away, come away with William Tell'. Those two songs he really knew well – it was something he enjoyed. He would sit on the swings and sing them even when he was an adult. So other bairns used to make a fool of him – 'cause he was an adult playing on swings – shouting at him. We had to fight the other kids over him. We had real scraps because of him.

When my grandad was ill, my father sent me to live with him. I was almost seventeen. There was my auntie Maggie, my uncle, my granny and grandad. All four of them were ill, and my grandfather was really ill, so I had a handful, a real handful, you know what I mean? I had no help. I had to wash my uncle, shave him. I mind he used to say, "Dinnae cut, dinnae cut," because it was razors them days. I had to help my granny out of bed because she'd had strokes and auntie Maggie, she wasn't as bad as my uncle but she wisnae all there either. But she could cope. So I had the whole lot, and I was seventeen, I didn't really like it that responsibility for the whole family, and no help, but they wouldnae take help.

Always the women, mind, who are caring. My daughter would send her daughter to me for example. Like when I had the stroke I couldnae get up in the morning, I had to lie in bed. I was in a caravan, I couldnae get out of bed, so she had to come over and lift bunks, clean the trailer, cook and clean, and this went on for months.

See us Travellers when you're married, you like to keep your own trailer, so they'd have their own home but still want to be close to help me. But nope, the council won't allow it. So, what's older Travellers supposed to do? It gets called 'doubling up' but it's no allowed here. Some sites it is though; you can have your family staying for a limited period. In this area, they built this site and stopped. Where's the young ones to go? There's nowhere for them to stay. Take my granddaughter. She went to a private site and she was refused because she was a Gypsy/Traveller. She was putting her jacks down on her trailer and the woman came over and said, "You'll have to move 'cause you're a Gypsy/Traveller."

But she said, "I'm nae moving the night."

The woman replied, "You'll have to move tomorrow, you can go down to the moor." So the moor was good enough for her but not a caravan site. How can you win in this society?

There's laws that make it illegal but they're not getting fulfilled, we got ethnic status, got the culture and that recognised but still there is discrimination. I think that makes it racism against Travellers on the part of the Government: they turn a blind eye. So now can you understand why Travellers have kept everything to themselves for years?

I'm straight upfront and I don't care who hears me or what I've got to say, freedom of speech. To me it's like the suffragettes, chaining themselves to the railings to be heard. Is that what the Travellers have to dae?

Margaret McKenzie

A Gypsy/Traveller camp in Fife

Driving Licence

When I got my driving licence, aw it was like a ticket to freedom. The world was my oyster when I got this.

Jolene

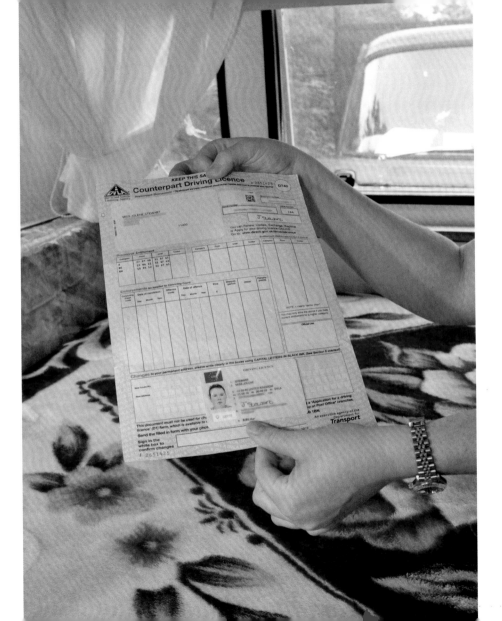

This House Is Killing Me

I've been a trainer and volunteer for many years. What we try to do is raise awareness about the issues we face and the prejudice that's still in Scotland today. Doing the training has not only learnt me loads, but has helped me keep positive mental health. But at first it was like going against your own because it was, "Why are you mixing with those people because they are the very same people as are putting us down?" That's what it was like to our own people. Even now some are saying, "What are you doing?"

It's to get a voice, to give my opinion, not just anybody's opinion but my opinion, my experiences, and to know that I can speak to people on my terms, not just on their terms. Any decisions that's ever been made about Gypsy/Travellers, has been from people that's never been involved with them or seen or know how we live. I've stayed on sites where the council has got funding for to do up the sites and I've seen changes but not for the sites, for our lifestyle, but changes for the council and their workers to come on site.

In the seminars we cover prejudices and bad practice. There is some good practice but unfortunately not a lot of it. The most important bit of the training is our input, our personal life stories, so to speak, and we are confident about speaking about them because obviously we've lived them, so we're not reading from books or papers.

We need more seminars because as much as our lives are not getting any easier, it's also helping us access services to make our lifestyles healthier. Such as trying to get to doctors when we need them. Knowing that when we can't get registered, we don't have to accept that, which I have done in the past; I have driven hundreds of miles for doctors.

The training needs to be compulsory within certain levels of professional people, such as at least one person in every school or health centre. There's genuine people out there that's willing to help and we meet

them through seminars and numbers get passed on, services get passed on, which don't always help me, but I'm going to pass them on to somebody else they're going to help. Word of mouth is better than anything else in the Travelling community. It's a trust issue, isn't it?

If you are fed up, or depressed, or anxious and you go to a doctor that doesn't understand Travelling People, for to walk in there and say, "I'm really, really fed up," and they ask you the reasons why. For to turn round and say, "I'm fed up because this house is killing me, this house has made me feel ..." They don't understand how the house can be folding in on top of you and suffocating you. That's a very, very real problem among Travelling People today, being imprisoned in a house. It's a very real issue. Because in their eyes, in their opinion, you'd be better off in a house than in a caravan. But why, because a caravan is normal to us?

Nowadays, we're going onto these sites and houses, there is so much separation going on. I mean it's totally different from being at the side of the road. The difference is very dramatic and going from a site into a house is even worse. On the side of the road it's going back to the old ways. The way it should be. It's where you could be living in gutters to your knees and be very happy because you don't have the security cameras, the wardens. I feel safer sitting at the side of the road than I do sitting in this house because you've got your family around you – you know who's beside you. The children's well looked after; they have their boundaries and so much more respect for their elders and who's around them. Everybody's catered for and cared for and nobody goes without. And if somebody is unwell, then everybody will take turns looking after them.

These sites and houses is separating families. That's the glue that Travelling People needs, it's the family. In these sites you're segregated, segregated from the world, segregated from your own kind of people. If you take ill, you can't invite your mother or your sister to come and stay with you because you're not allowed an extra caravan on the plot. At the side of the road you can have anybody you want staying beside you or staying in your home. We're a community and part of that is being lost moving from camps to sites, and it's even worse leaving sites to come into houses – when you shut that door that's the end of it. You could be sat in your house for weeks, months and you don't see any-body. There's my wee lassie – she's away and married now – ultimately she should be beside me, especially now. If we were on roadside camps she would be beside me, I wouldnae have lost her as such, but I have because I'm in a house and she's went back to a caravan. How ironic is that!

Years ago when my children were in the schooling system, if anything happened at

Georgia McCann and her daughter at a training event

the school I would just wipe my hands of it and take my children out of school and that was it. Ultimately they were the ones that missed out.

Then when I started doing the seminars, I demanded meetings at schools, to speak to head teachers, I demanded answers. I suppose my confidence grew with dealing with the services, not all of them, but trust, trust just grew. I know that I can speak to a police officer without being demeaned,

I know I can stand there and speak and actually say, "No you can't speak to me like that, you can't do that." When I say that, it was only last year that I was actually refused access to a holiday site. So we had been on the site the year before – a holiday site. We stayed there kept everything tidy – we had the camper van. I think that made a difference in itself. The man knew when he let us on exactly what we were because the man was used to Travelling People. Not that we blatantly showed it, but he knew. We got on and stayed there, paid our electric, paid our rent faithfully. Children was kept in about, everything was kept clean, dog was tied up. Shook hands with the man and said thanks for letting us stay.

In the month of February got a letter from the council offering us a seasonal stance which lasts from March till October. So the offer was there: we could pay up front and go and stay for all these months, but because of my own circumstances I said no at that time. Then later we decided to go and went straight to the warden's office and he was really sort of arrogant towards us. I asked if we could get on and he said, "No. You're not allowed on," and I said, "But why? I want a reason," and he said, "You're not getting on." So I said, "Is it because of who I am?" I just wanted him to say it but he wouldn't. We were in the wee office and when these holidaymakers came in behind me I was so embarrassed, I was on the verge of tears. So I said, "I'm no getting anywhere with you, am I?" I knew for a candid fact that there were Travelling People on that specific ground at that time, I knew that. They weren't disguising who they were, they had their watering cans outside and everything. I just came out the office and said, "We'll see about this!" and the holidaymakers just moved up the queue and were allocated their pitch.

So I phoned the council and advised them I was reporting in a racial incident that had happened to me. And there wasn't any sort of response, so I explained what had happened and I said that I was continuing with this complaint. They said they would phone me back and they did – they said they had sorted it out, that it had been a misunderstanding and I could go and pull on the site. But I was warned not to have any repercussions with the caretaker. I said, "What do you mean repercussions?" and they said they didn't want any repercussions for what had just happened 'cause he's doing his job. I said, "Is that right? As a rule I'm not an angry person, I don't know why you would say that to me."

So when we went to pull on, the man's face was like thunder and he started being really cheeky with me. So I said, "I've been asked not to have any repercussions with you so I'm not going to speak badly to you, I'm not going to lose my temper with you and I expect the same respect in return," and because I spoke properly to him and

used words with him, he just couldn't believe that I had the knowledge to do such a thing. He couldn't believe what had happened. By that time I didn't want to go on the site but I went on just to prove my point, and I thought there's going to be repercussions obviously going over his head and whatever. And he apologised to my husband but he never ever apologised to me. He just said, "I am sorry for not letting you on but I was just doing my job. I was told not to let you on. None of yous." But he wouldn't say outright what it was, so it's a case of being discriminated against but having no proof because the words were just not there. It goes back to the old story: they can still discriminate without even using the words.

Ten or fifteen years ago I would have stood, I would have screamed, I would have shouted, I would have got absolutely nowhere and the man would probably have felt intimidated and probably the police would have been

Georgia, Alex Salmond MSP (First Minister of Scotland) and Lizzie Johnstone

called because I would probably just have said, "I'm not leaving!" This would have got nobody anywhere and I would have got in trouble just to try and get on the holiday site. But I know that I don't have to put up with that, I know that I can speak and I know that it is discrimination. I know how hard it is to prove still, even now. To threaten that you

are going to report them, that carries a wee bit of weight. Not a lot but a wee bit. For us discrimination is still very real, it's still going on, and as a trainer, going to these seminars, it goes against everything I believe in for to let it go over my head and put up with it.

My long-term aims are to introduce more trainers, so that we can have more seminars and that we can encourage the younger ones. Because as much as I go through the discrimination, I know I can take it, but the younger ones, they need their confidence built and to be educated as to how to deal with these issues.

Georgia McCann

Are You Sitting Comfortably?

Are you sitting comfortably
Are you listening
Are you awake
Please take notes
I really don't mind
I am a Traveller
I am a mother
I am a full-time carer
To my son

It hasn't always been easy
In fact I can say
It's been a nightmare
At times over the years
I have felt frustrated
I have felt isolated
I have felt suffocated
No-one taking
Any notice or understanding
How I am feeling
Like an animal trapped in a cage
Screaming to get out

Why can't someone show compassion
And realise I need help
To figure out even my son's medication
As I can't read or write
It's not my fault I am only doing my best
Thought I made the right decision
Moving into a house
Giving up my culture
And ways of life
So my son
Could get the proper health care he was entitled to
Like everyone else
For God's sake
Please don't let other Travellers
Suffer the way I had to.

Lizzie Johnstone wrote this poem for, and read it aloud when she gave evidence to, the Scottish Parliament Equal Opportunities Committee Gypsy/Travellers and Care Inquiry. It was first published in their official report, 15 May 2012, Col. 407.

Glossary

aboot – about

arenae – are not, aren't

aroon – around

aye – yes, always

aw – all, everything

awfy – very, awful, awfully

bairns – children

barry – fine, big, smart in appearance

BBM – instant messaging service

blades – knives

bobble – small plastic balls attached to a circular piece of elastic, used for fastening girls' hair.

bonny – beautiful, pretty

cannae – cannot, can't

couldnae – could not, couldn't

claes – clothes

da – father, dad

daddy-long-legs – crane fly

dae – do

di – die

didnae – did not, didn't

dinnae – do not, don't

disnae – does not, doesn't

doon – down

fae – from

feared – afraid, fearful

fer – to

gadgie – man especially non-Gypsy/Traveller

gaunie – going to

gie – give

gied – gave

grandwean – grandchild

gutters – mud, mire, muddy puddles

hadnae – had not, hadn't

hame – home

havenae – have not, haven't

heap/heaps – a large amount or number of

heid – head

hoose – house

ken – know, knowledge

laddie – boy

lassie – girl

learnt – taught

lecy – electricity

lift – arrest

ma – my

mair – more

mammy – mother

masel – myself

mind – remember

mooth – mouth
muffler – a scarf, usually worn around the neck
        or head
nae – no, none
naebody – nobody
neeps – turnips
no – not
o'er – over
oot – out
ootside – outside
pull on – set up camp
Rest and Be Thankful – part of the A83 road
        at the top of Glen Croe
ringtails – rats
roo – round, around
roond – round
scaldie – person who lives in a house
skelp – slap, strike, hit
tae – to, too, toe
tatties – potatoes
telt – told
the day – today
they – the, those
took – taken
toon – town

totie – tiny
trailer – caravan
wasnae – was not, wasn't
weans – children (often pronounced wains)
wee – small, short
werenae – were not, weren't
wi' – with
windae – window
wis – was
wisnae – was not, wasn't
wouldnae – would not, wouldn't
yabbing – harping on a subject, talking incessantly
ye – you
yous – you
yon – that

Plates

Cover photograph: A85 approaching Tyndrum. Peter E Ross 2012 .

The Chattery photographs on pages:

12/18/27/32/39/45/54/63/68/78/86/93/99/105/117/120/127 by Peter E Ross.

p2	Patsy Stewart Hilton. Peter E Ross 2012.
p5	Dad (John Robertson Stewart), Benny and mum (Maggie Stewart), Perth. Family archive mid-1960s.
p7	Benny Stewart. Family archive 2009.
p9	By Invitation Only. Watercolour. Shamus McPhee 2003.
p15	Fiona MacDonald. Peter E Ross 2013.
p16	Margaret and Fiona MacDonald. Peter E Ross 2013.
p20	Double Dykes Caravan Site, Perth. Peter E Ross 2012.
p22	Gypsy/Traveller camp near Perth. The Scotsman 1960s.
p23	Gypsy/Traveller camp Inveralmond near Perth. A.D.S. Macpherson 1964.
p24	Fiona Townsley with some of her correspondence and research papers. Peter E Ross 2012.
p28	Tom 'Winky' Devers. Peter E Ross 2012.
p30	Gypsy/Travellers on the road, Scottish Borders. Peter E Ross 1995.
p34	Betsy MacDonald. Peter E Ross 2012.
p35	Betsy MacDonald with Ashley and Shannon. Family archive 2002.
p36	William MacDonald (jnr) with turtle at Tobermory, Isle of Mull. Family archive 1998.
p41	Susan Townsley on the lift into her chalet, Double Dykes, Perth. Peter E Ross 2012.
p42	Roseanna McPhee. Peter E Ross 2012.
p46	Libby's daughter Mirren MacDonald. Peter E Ross 2013.
p48	Ledaig Site, Argyll. Peter E Ross 2013.
p49	Libby Brown. Peter E Ross 2013.
p53	Thomas Stewart and his restored pickup truck. Peter E Ross 2012.
p56	Kathy McGuigan's family (the Townsleys) in front of their horse-drawn wagon in England. Family archive 1976.
p57	Kathy's mum (Maggie Townsley) in Ullapool. Family archive mid-1980s.
p59	Kathy and her mum in Dunkeld. Family archive 1990s.
p65	Charlene MacDonald and Kieran. Peter E Ross 2013.
p66	Charlene MacDonald's poem. Peter E Ross 2013.

p67   Ledaig Site, Argyll. Peter E Ross 2013.

p70   Isa Johnstone in her mother's (Isabella) arms next to Jeannie McCallum and others at Arrochar. William (Willie) Webb 1938.

p71   Granny Belle (Belle Johnstone) on Pitlochry Bridge. Unknown photographer circa 1940.

p72   Isa Johnstone. Peter E Ross 2012.

p73   Anthony Stewart. Family archive 1940s.

p77   Gypsy/Traveller camp, South Queensferry. Peter E Ross 1999.

p80   Edith Townsley. Peter E Ross 2013.

p83   Edith's brother in his trailer. Family archive 1990s.

p89   Betty Irvine's mum, Betty, in the centre and aunt Bella to her right. Family archive circa 1960.

p90   Betty Irvine's dad, Ginger, Uncle Oney and her dad's nieces Violet, Thomasina and Rose. Family archive circa 1960.

p94   David McDonald. Peter E Ross 2012.

p95   David McDonald visiting his mother, Catherine, in hospital, Lochgilphead. Family archive 2011.

p96   David McDonald on the shores of Loch Etive. Still from video *Hidden Carers. Unheard Voices.* Peter E Ross 2011.

p101   Martina Doherty. Peter E Ross 2013.

p102   Martina comforts her son as he undergoes more tests, Royal Hospital for Sick Children, Edinburgh. Peter E Ross 2013.

p107   Paradise Lost. Oil on canvas. Shamus McPhee 2003.

p108   Big Chill At Bobbin Mill. Oil on board. Shamus McPhee 2003.

p109   Los Desaparecidos. Oil on board. Shamus McPhee 2003.

p111   Maggie Townsley visits Jeanie in her caravan. Peter E Ross 2012.

p112   Maggie Townsley. Peter E Ross 2012.

p114   Touch. Peter E Ross 2012.

p119   Pipers at Birnam. Photographer unknown 1898.

p122   Margaret McKenzie, with bow, and her sisters Doreen, in the centre, and Sandra, on the right. Family archive circa 1960.

p125   Gypsy/Traveller camp, Fife. Peter E Ross circa 1998.

p129   Georgia McCann. Peter E Ross 2013.

p131   Georgia McCann and her daughter at a training event. MECOPP 2013.

p134   Georgia McCann, Alex Salmond MSP (First Minister of Scotland) and Lizzie Johnstone outside the Scottish Parliament. McCann family archive 2013.